STOP.
AF604606
YAY!

YAY!

SHOUTS THE EXCLAMATION MARK

BY ROB LISLE

First Published 2026 by
Redback Publishing
Suite 6, 13a Narabang Way,
Belrose NSW 2085
Australia

www.redbackpublishing.com
orders@redbackpublishing.com

ISBN ISBN 978-1-761402-11-1

Author: Rob Lisle
Editor: Simone Saba
Designer: Redback Publishing
Illustrator: Rob Lisle

Originated by Redback Publishing

A catalogue record for this book is available from the National Library of Australia

CAN YOU SPOT HELMET HENRICK IN EVERY SPREAD?

YAY!
SHOUTS THE EXCLAMATION MARK

Exclamation marks are very handy. They can show **surprise** or **shock**.

My goodness!
Ahh!
FRUIT
My fruit!
spedsy
Hellooo!
oooooo!
Hear ye! Hear ye!
Water is so yummy!

Greetings!
Hey, chicken!
Oi!
Bok!
Yo!
Ahoy there!
Hey, Ragnar!
Yoo hoo!

Exclamation marks can show someone is calling out for **attention** or **help**.
Help me!
Hello!
Attention, men!
Attention!
Let me show you my flipper slap trick!

Exclamation marks can show **excitement** or **joy**.

They're back!
Welcome home!
Finally!
I'm so happy to see you all!
Oink!
Yahoo!
Oink!

Exclamation marks can even show **love**.
Yes! Fresh apples!
I love you two!
We missed you so much!
You're home!

You guys are so cute!
Smells good!
Oink! Oink!
Squeak!
Bok! Bok!

Exclamation marks can show **urgency**.

Sir! We've found something you might like!
Ba-gok!
Look out! Coming through!
The kitchen is on fire!
I can't wait to eat!
HEY! I can't see!

AH!
WOOOSH!
CHEEP!
BOK!
CHEEP!
HNN!
THUD!
BONK!

Exclamation marks can show **loud noises**.

Exclamation marks can be used to express **anger** or **frustration**.
It's so much further than I thought!
Oh, stop your moaning!
You stop moaning about my moaning!
Both of you be quiet and row!
Bok!
Cheep!

Faster, you slowpokes!
Bok!
Ahh, this is so annoying!
I can't see where we're going!
Grr!

Go away!
Squawk!
Turn around and go home!
Come on in!
Get out of here!
Give us all your gold!
Bring the ladder!

Exclamation marks can be used to give a **command** or make a **strong request**.
No fighting!
Squawk!
Bok!
Oink!
You can't park there. Move!
Squawk!
Keep going!
Lift it higher!
Watch out!

Sometimes you may need to use an exclamation mark to **make your point** very clear.
We have a deal!
Giant is friend!
Run!
Bok!

We do indeed!
Friends forever!
Squawk!

Whether it is a **yell**, a **holler** or a **hoot** – an exclamation mark can give a sentence a little **pop!**
You've got something on your head!
Squeak!
Hey!
Bok!
Get down from there!
Cheers to all!
ZZZ
ZZZ

Bok!
Peace in the realm at last!
Finally!
Hello new friends!
Moo!
So happy to be home!
Let's dance!
Oink!
ZZZ

You might use repeated exclamation marks to show **extreme excitement** or **enthusiasm**.

NOT YET!

Now that you're an EXCLAMATION MARK master, use your new skills to give these characters a voice!
Tell us what these characters are thinking! SHOUT it out loud!
!
!
!

!
Flip back through the book to find these scenes.
!
!
!
!

ACTIVITIES

SPOT THE EXCLAMATION!

OBJECTIVE	To identify when an exclamation mark is needed in sentences.
STEPS	• Provide a list of sentences with or without exclamation marks. • Have kids read each sentence and decide if it needs an exclamation mark or not. • If it needs an exclamation mark, they should write it at the end of the sentence. If not, leave it as is.
BONUS ACTIVITY	After completing the task, read the sentences aloud with exaggerated emotion to practise the feeling behind the punctuation.

EXAMPLE SENTENCES

"I can't believe it."

"Wow, look at that!"

"Hooray, we won!"

FEEL THE EMOTION!

OBJECTIVE	To understand the emotion behind exclamation marks.
STEPS	• Have kids create a list of emotions like excitement, surprise, happiness and anger. • For each emotion, write a sentence that shows the emotion and ends with an exclamation mark.
BONUS ACTIVITY	Have kids act out the emotions while reading their sentences out loud, using different tones and expressions to match each feeling.

EXAMPLES

Excitement: "We've got treasures!"

Surprise: "Those are really big toes!"

Anger: "Ahh, this is so annoying!"

Happiness: "I'm so happy to see you all!"

CREATE YOUR OWN EXCLAMATION SENTENCES!

OBJECTIVE

To create sentences that use exclamation marks properly.

STEPS

- Kids are to create their own Viking character.
- Ask them to select five pages from the book and write on a separate piece of paper what their Viking would exclaim in that scenario.
- Their exclamation should be original and match the emotion of the page.

EXAMPLES

To call for attention my Viking would say:

"Oi there! I'm coming to rescue you!"

To express surprise my Viking would say:

"Wow! I can't believe we beat the giant!"

BONUS ACTIVITY

Children can draw their Viking on a poster or piece of paper and depict what they are doing in each of the scenes.

EXCLAMATION MARK MATCH-UP

OBJECTIVE

To match emotions or actions to the correct use of an exclamation mark.

STEPS

- Provide a list of emotions or actions and a list of sentences without punctuation.
- Have kids match the emotion/action with the sentence that needs an exclamation mark.

EXAMPLE EMOTIONS/ ACTIONS	SENTENCES
Happiness	"I love you two!"
Demanding	"The kitchen is on fire!"
Love	"You can't park there! Move!"
Urgency	"So happy to be home!"

BONUS ACTIVITY

Have kids act out the emotions and shout the sentences aloud with enthusiasm.

SHOUT OUT CHALLENGE!

OBJECTIVE	To encourage kids to use exclamation marks in a creative and fun way.
STEPS	• Have the children come up with five things from the book that made them excited, surprised or happy. • For each item on their list, they should write an exclamation sentence about it.
EXAMPLE	"I found Helmet Henrick!" "I want to be a Viking!" "The giant is back!"
BONUS ACTIVITY	Have a mini 'Shout Out' session where kids can read their exclamation-filled sentences to the class or group.

EXCLAMATION MARK COMIC STRIP

OBJECTIVE	To understand how exclamation marks work in storytelling.
STEPS	• Provide kids with a simple 4-panel comic strip template. • Ask them to design their own Viking and fill in the speech bubbles with sentences that use exclamation marks to show excitement, surprise or a strong emotion.
BONUS ACTIVITY	Have the children present their comic strips to the class or family, emphasising the use of exclamation marks through expressive reading.

EXAMPLES

Panel 1: Viking Ragnar discovers a hole in his boat.	Panel 2: Viking Ragnar exclaims, "Oh no! My boat is going to sink!"
Panel 3: Viking Freya says, "I can help you fix it!"	Panel 4: Freya and Ragnar work on the boat. Ragnar says, "You're the best!"

NARRATIVE TEXT

The Viking crew set sail in search of gold and wealth. They sailed right up to the docks of the Red Kingdom, hoping to do what Vikings do best.

They were planning to invade!

The red kingdom's guards were already waiting at the gates. "Turn around and go home!" they called. There was no way they were going to let the Vikings through!

"Give us your gold!" demanded the Vikings' leader.

"Bring the ladder!" his wife commanded to the crew as they prepared to climb the walls.

"Go away!" shouted the Red Kingdom's king.

The tension was rising between the Vikings and knights; they shouted at each other from the boat and the city walls.

It looks like they might all get in a fight!

EXCLAMATION MARK DETECTIVE

OBJECTIVE

To practise identifying exclamation marks in different texts.

STEPS

- Have the kids read the short narrative, depicting a scene from the book.
- Ask them to underline every sentence that uses an exclamation mark.
- Have them rewrite the sentence to show how adding and removing exclamation marks changes the meaning of the sentence.

EXAMPLE

Original:
"Go away!"

Rewritten:
"Go away."

BONUS ACTIVITY

The children can select a page and write their own short narrative based on the scene. Tell them to include exclamation marks where fitting in their prose, and use the speech bubbles from the scene.

COLLECT ALL THE BOOKS IN THE PUNCTUATION EXPEDITION SERIES!

WAIT,
HUH?